THE CHRISTMAS STRANGER

A One-act Christmas Play

BY CHARLES W. BYRD

C.S.S. Publishing Co., Inc.
Lima, Ohio

THE CHRISTMAS STRANGER

Scripture quotations are from the *New Revised Standard Version of the Bible*,
copyright 1989 by the Division of Christian Education of the National Council of
the Churches of Christ in the USA. Used by permission.

9248 / ISBN 1-55673-453-0   PRINTED IN U.S.A.

Therefore the Lord himself will give you a sign. Look, the young woman is with child and shall bear a son, and shall name him Immanuel.

— Isaiah 7:14

Production Notes

This simple play is easily adaptable for any size group, or any ratio of male-female parts. Either a stage or the choir-altar area of the church may be used. No special props or costumes are required, other than a lectern and a Bible.

Characters

Mrs. Black, leader of the group.

(These names may be revised if necessary)
    Bill
    Janet
    James
    Karen
    Bill
    Jenny
    Harold
    Lucy
    Len
    Carol

First Mr. Carpenter

Second Mr. Carpenter

The Christmas Stranger

(The church youth group and their adult leader are in the altar-choir area preparing to practice for their Christmas program.)

Mrs. Black: Come on, gang. Take your places for practice. It isn't long till our Christmas program and we're still having some difficulty with our music. We'll try *(Suggestion: "Come, Thou Long-Expected Jesus" or "Savior Of The Nations, Come")* first.

(The youth group takes its place)

(song)

Mrs. Black: That sounds much better, but some of you don't seem very enthusiastic. Bill, you look a little glum. Is anything wrong?

Bill: Well, Mrs. Black, I don't mean to be disagreeable, but I just can't help but wonder why we're having a Christmas program at all. I mean, well, my dad says that with all the problems in the world, it's a little silly for people to go in for all this Christmas stuff.

Mrs. Black: Why, Bill, I'm sure your father believes in Christmas. Maybe you two just haven't gotten the Christmas spirit yet.

Janet: I think I understand what Bill means, Mrs. Black. Here we are planning a program about love and peace when there's so much fighting and hatred in the world.

James: That's right! I read in the paper today that another Middle East war might break out at any minute . . . . *(Any current news headline could be substituted here.)*

Karen: And I saw on the television news that crime in our city alone has increased 12 percent over last year!

John: And what about the homeless?

Bill: Yes, and let's not forget the problems we're having in our own church!

Jenny: Can you imagine! Grown people who call themselves Christians arguing over whether to buy a new organ or new carpeting!

Harold: Yeah, and my mother was right in the thick of the fight, too.

Lucy:	But at least it wasn't *your* mother who threw the pitcher of water in the board chairperson's face. I'll never, never live that down!
John:	Neither will the chairperson!
Len:	I'll never forget the look on Mr. Ferguson's face when that water hit him! My father said he hadn't seen anybody that surprised since the preacher dropped the communion wine in Mrs. Wilson's lap!

(All laugh)

Mrs. Black:	Hold it, gang! I agree with you that there are many problems in the world and that Christians do not always act as they should. But, does that not prove the *need* for Christmas programs — with the emphasis upon our Lord's birth and life? Through activities such as ours, the love of God can be expressed and the spirit of Christ will have an opportunity to change the lives of people.
Group Response:	Well, yes . . . I suppose so . . . I guess you're right . . .
Bill:	Maybe . . . but I'm not so sure . . .
Mrs. Black:	We'll talk about it more, later, but for now we'd better get on with the practice. The trustees hired a new custodian today and he'll be in soon to clean and lock up the church. Let's try . . . *(A solo is suggested here.)*

(Just as the song ends the door opens and a man enters. He seems to be in his 30s, with plain, somewhat worn clothing.)

13

Mrs. Black: We'll be through in a few minutes, Mr. Carpenter. Do you mind waiting?

Mr. Carpenter: Not at all, Mrs. Black. I'll just sit here and listen. *(He sits down.)*

Mrs. Black: Thank you, Mr. Carpenter. Carol, are you ready to read your scriptures concerning Christ?

Carol: I'm — I'm sorry, Mrs. Black. I went to a basketball game last night and I guess I just forgot to look them up.

Mrs. Black: Oh . . . Well, I suppose we can leave them until next Sunday's practice, but they were so important . . .

Mr. Carpenter: Excuse me, Mrs. Black. I don't mean to interfere, but I'm somewhat familiar with the Bible and I would be happy to read for you. I'm sure I could find some appropriate passages.

Mrs. Black: Why, thank you, Mr. Carpenter. That would be very helpful.

(Mr. Carpenter stands at lectern, opens the Bible and begins to read.)

Mr. Carpenter: Therefore the Lord himself will give you a sign. Look, the young woman is with child and shall bear a son, and shall name him Immanuel (Isaiah 7:14).

For a child has been born for us, a son given to us; authority rests upon his shoulders;

and he is named Wonderful Counselor, Mighty God, Everlasting Father, Prince of Peace. His authority shall grow continually, and there shall be endless peace for the throne of David and his kingdom. He will establish and uphold it with justice and with righteousness from this time onward and forevermore (Isaiah 9:6-7).

Awake, awake, put on your strength, O Zion! Put on your beautiful garments, O Jerusalem, the holy city . . . How beautiful upon the mountains are the feet of the messenger who announces peace, who brings good news, who announces salvation, who says to Zion, "Your God reigns." Listen! Your sentinels lift up their voices, together they sing for joy; for in plain sight they see the return of the Lord to Zion. Break forth together into singing, you ruins of Jerusalem; for the Lord has comforted his people, he has redeemed Jerusalem. The Lord has bared his holy arm before the eyes of all the nations; and all the ends of the earth shall see the salvation of our God (Isaiah 52:1, 7-10).

(Mr. Carpenter pauses and the group begins to sing. Suggestion: "O Little Town Of Bethlehem" or "Infant Holy, Infant Lowly")

Mr. Carpenter: Then Jesus grew, and one day as a young man he began to preach and teach, saying: Blessed are they which do hunger and thirst after righteousness; for they shall be filled. Blessed are the merciful; for they shall obtain mercy. Blessed are the pure in heart; for they shall

15

see God. Blessed are the peacemakers; for they shall be called the children of God.

You are the light of the world. A city that is set upon a hill cannot be hidden. Neither do men light a candle and put it under a basket, but on a candlestick; and it gives light unto all who are in the house. Let your light shine before all people, that they may see your good works, and glorify your Father who is in heaven.

You have heard that it has been said, "You shall love your neighbor, but hate your enemy." But I say to you, Love your enemies, bless them that curse you, do good to them who hate you, and pray for them who despitefully use you and persecute you; that you may be the children of your Father who is in heaven; for he makes his sun to shine on the evil and the good, and sends rain on the just and the unjust. Be you therefore perfect, even as your Father who is in heaven is perfect.

Come unto me all you that labor and are heavy laden, and I will give you rest. Take my yoke upon you, and learn of me; for I am meek and lowly of heart; and you shall find rest for your souls.

I am the resurrection and the life; he that believes on me, though he were dead, yet shall he live; and whosoever lives and believes in me shall never die (Matthew paraphrased).

(Mr. Carpenter pauses. The group softly sings. Suggestion: "O For A Thousand Tongues To Sing" or "My Jesus, I Love Thee")

Mr. Carpenter: A new commandment I give you, that you love one another; as I have loved you, that you also love one another.

If you love me, keep my commandments. And I will pray the Father, and he shall give you another Comforter, that he may abide with you forever. Peace I give you, my peace I give to you; not as the world gives, give I to you. Let not your heart be troubled, neither let it be afraid.

I am the resurrection and the life, and lo! I am with you always, even unto the end of the world . . .

(After the reading there is a moment of silence)

Mrs. Black: Thank you, Mr. Carpenter. I don't believe I have ever heard those words read more meaningfully.

Mr. Carpenter: I hope I have been of some help. I must be on with my work now. *(He goes to the door, pauses, smiles slightly at the group, then exits.)*

Mrs. Black: *(Calling after him)* We'll be finished in a few minutes, Mr. Carpenter. Bill, I wonder if those scriptures don't answer the questions you raised earlier.

Bill: Yes, Mrs. Black. I think I understand the real meaning of Christmas now.

(There is a knock on the door. It opens and a strange man comes in.)

Stranger: Good evening. I'm Mr. Carpenter, the new custodian.

Mrs. Black: *You're* Mr. Carpenter! But there was another man here a moment ago who said . . . no, he didn't really *say* he was Mr. Carpenter, but I assumed he was. But — *who* was he?

Mr. Carpenter: I don't know about that, ma'am, but I know that *I'm* George Carpenter, the new custodian.

Mrs. Black: You must have passed the other man as you came in, didn't you?

Mr. Carpenter: No, ma'am, I didn't pass anybody. I don't mean to hurry you, but I'd sure like to clean and lock up soon.

Mrs. Black: All right, Mr. Carpenter . . . but I don't understand . . . who was he . . .?

Youth: *(Several voices)* Who do you think he was? Where did he go? Mrs. Black, who was he?

Mrs. Black: *(Hesitantly)* I don't know . . . surely it couldn't be . . . he was probably just a stranger who wandered in out of the cold. And yet, he called me by name . . . oh well, we can discuss it later. But now let us sing our last song.

(Song suggestion: "Hark The Herald Angels Sing" or "Angels From The Realms Of Glory")

The End